ROLE OF COMPETITION REGULATORS IN THE DOMAIN OF DATA PRIVACY

VOLUME 2, ISSUE 3 OF BRILLOPEDIA

DANISH CHANDRA

Made with ❤ on the Notion Press Platform
www.notionpress.com

Contents

Preface

"Start writing, no matter what. The water does not flow until the faucet is turned on".

• Louis L'Amour

Hundreds of students and professors are contributing their work to Brillopedia, we are here to provide ample information about Law and Contemporary issues. Our aim is to provide a platform for today's generation to express their views and ideas on law and contemporary law.

Publication

This research paper is published in volume 2, issue 3 of Brillopedia

CHAPTER ONE

ABSTRACT

There have been tremendous growth of technology and digital business models in the past decade and especially during the recent pandemic years in India and worldwide. While this growth has led to the emergence of many new business models, and new market options to the consumers, it has also raised concerns about the digital influence and the privacy of user's data in the competitive digital market. In this context, many bodies or organizations have started to amend the traditional concerns of the competition regulation amid the digital business models. However, there are at early stages and the current role of competition regulators lack at many aspects. This article focuses on the role of competition regulators in the domain of data privacy and briefly covers the role and need of competition law, competition regulation and how it is linked to the domain of data privacy. The objective of this article is to shed some light on the current laws available on the competition regulation for data privacy, their limitations and some case studies in this area along with the future possibilities.

CHAPTER TWO

INTRODUCTION

Competition regulators are constituent of law, economics and politics to provide an unfair means of competition in market.[1]The competition law in digital media and data privacy is founded on five pillars constituting data portability, interoperability, and implementation of data portability and interoperability and implementation of legal aids involving anti-trust regulatory framework and public policy development. In India the both the data portability and interoperability are regulated in maintained to create a harmony in competition market, by Competition Commission of India (CCI).[2]The Indian Competition Act, 2002 was established for a robust framework supported by section 21 and section 21A providing the CCI full authority to establish the competition law in Indian market. "The competition law review committee further added to broaden the scope of CCI and remove any kind of contradiction or conflicts that could arise in the market". [3]Furthermore, the government of India added the "Competition (Amendment) Bill, 2020" that was put forward in common public for consulting or any changes.

CCI is the market regulator powered by jurisdiction of India across all the sectors of economy. The competition regulators have a significant role in regulating the data privacy and management. Online enterprises have emerged more significantly in the recent years and specifically amid the pandemic situation. [4]The use of consumer data allows the business models to develop data driven services and innovations leading to more profit and value. This holds a twofold value since it also benefits the consumers to be able to get better access to the products of their interest and better upgrades and services. [5]A data abundant environment is able to enhance the competitive market in terms of their services and target oriented for its customers. The companies may however use the data to their advantage by develop targeted services based on user preferences and additional funding to attract more network pool of users and services often referred to as the monetization feedback loop. They further have capacity to convert the data access to entry prohibition in digital market. Hereby, "the anti-trust law" was set up to provide as an additional regulating tool in tackling the unscrupulous and consumptive behaviour of the influential companies in the data accumulation and date storage. Further light was shed to the matter by the "Market Study Report on the telecom sector in [6]India issued by the CCI recently in January, 2021" to focus on the relation between the data privacy and the competition regulation. The details of the report are discussed in the later sections along with the role of competition regulators and their need.

CHAPTER THREE

COMPETITION REGULATORS

Competition regulators acts as an organizational body governing the business market trailing the competition law established in 1969 as "Monopolies and Restrictive Trade Practice Act (MRTP) later replaced by Competition Act, 2002" in India. In India, the "CCI (Competition Commission of India)" holds down the responsibility of ensuring the competition regulations and safeguards the philosophy and laws of competition act, 2002. [7]The anti-trust or competition law is founded on modern philosophy forbidding practice of anti-competitive agreements, abuse of power by influential corporations and businesses resulting to a dominant and monopoly status. Regulators may be either focused on some distinct zones or departments or may be national bodies whose objective is to implement nationwide competition laws fairly. [8]The sustainment of unbiased competition in the market allows a control of economy by the regulators. The competition regulators may be independent bodies depending on the nation's laws, these bodies have complete control over the private entities without any impact from the government or any other body. The independent bodies along with the competition authorities enforces merger control and anti-monopoly laws pertaining as the potent regulating institutions in maintaining the role of competition regulators and an efficacious and unfluctuating anti-trust policy all along the zones. The independent competition regulatory bodies are not obliged to perform the unnecessary anti-trust regulatory measures to accomplish its overall mission and purpose. Aided with other nonconventional and productive measures comprising intrusions to confront asymmetric data, confinement on the utilization of behavioural biases in addition to curtailing hindrances on entry and setting standards for portability wherever required. The implementation of competition regulators may vary in reference to the nation's policies and laws however the general objective and goal remains the same. The competition regulators worldwide and the competition regulators of India including the CCI objectives and ideology will be discussed in detail in the following sub-sections.

CHAPTER FOUR

NEED OF COMPETITION REGULATORS

The need of competition regulators arises with the purpose of competition laws, requisite to sustain the market from failures and malformations. [9]The use of dominance by powerful enterprises resorting to anti-competitive activities, misuse of dominance affecting the economic productivity and consumer well-being.Therefore, to protect the consumer from biased competition and enforce the best options for the common man and a fair opportunity to the producers in the market. The competition regulation is imperative to each including business so as to establish a productive efficiency and prohibit the poor management, incompetent work practices and superfluous waste in absence of a competitive environment. The need of competition law give rise to demand for competition regulators working as a constant monitor to implement and enforce competition laws. [10]Regulation shields the rightful concern of enterprises and the community. A robust flexible regulatory system assists the economy effectively and pliant as possible, also aiding in international economy competition.

However, in a fast-paced society the technology is more inclining towards the digital economy and data privacy followed by constant updates of business models and ideologies

COMPETITION REGULATORS AROUND THE WORLD

[11]Competition regulators are established all around the world by each distinct country according to their own jurisdictions and substantiating antitrust laws for protecting consumer rights. The complete list of all regulating bodies of the countries could be found at Federal Trade Commission (www.ftc.gov). The multinational regulatory organizations include European Commission Directorate General for Competition coupled with European Union, EFTA Surveillance Authority comprising Iceland, Norway and Liechtenstein and lastly the Communidad Andina inclusive for Andean Community of Nations. Some of the national regulators include:

1. Australia: "Australian competition and consumer commission established in 1995 in communion with Australian Trade Practice Commission"

2. Brazil: Administrative council for economic defense

3. Canada: Competition Bureau/Bureau de la concurrence

4. China: Ministry of Commerce

5. United Kingdom: Competition and Markets Authority

6. United States: Federal Trade Commission and US Department of Justice Antitrust Division

7. India: Competition Commission of India

8. Japan: Japan Fair Trade Commission

9. Russia: Federal Antimonopoly Service of Russia

10. South Korea: Federal Trade Commission

CHAPTER SIX

COMPETITION REGULATOR IN INDIA

The competition regulation is monitored by a statutory body under Ministry of Corporate Affairs of India namely the [12]Competition Commission of India (CCI) (www.cci.gov.in). CCI operates to promote and enforce antitrust laws and the Competition Act, 2002. [13]The main objective of this body is to prohibit any kind of dominance in competition or any other kind of adverse activity affecting the enterprise or consumer welfare. New Delhi-located CCI under the chairman Ashok Kumar Gupta has been established for 18 years now. Supreme Court of India in their judgment in [14]"Civil Appeal No 7999 of 2010" defined the objective of competition law in India "It encourages the economic effectiveness employing competition to contemplate admonitory in creation of market agile to consumer discretions. The privilege of competition is triplex: disbursement of resources, constructive effectiveness, thereby promoting minimum production cost and diversity in productivity, in addition to which innovative practice are encouraged".

CHAPTER SEVEN

ROLE OF COMPETITION REGULATORS IN DIGITAL SPACE AND DATA PRIVACY

Technological advancements in the digital sector have skyrocketed in India and worldwide. [15]The technical progression has directed the revolution of business models, establishment of new enterprises, and bulk movement of businesses towards digital platforms amid the pandemic in last two years. With the changing business models changed the data privacy concerns, for major enterprises such as Facebook which hold large amounts of user data may influence digital markets to their own benefits raising dominancy concerns.

The user data is collected in many distinctive ways which allows the distribution or selling of this data for profits and market failures. The data may be collected through online activities such as sensors, search interests, surveys, feedbacks, subscriptions, sensors involving IoT. The collected data is a huge set of raw data form accumulated through various activities one of the main factors involved in the increased use of data collection, theft, and privacy invasion is the improved data storages, facilities, and data analytics particularly after the innovation of cloud computing, and other techniques.

[16]The selling of user data information to third parties or other businesses has become a common practice either through user approval or in some cases misleading or hiding information from users for consent in data sharing or making it a mandatory step to access any service provided by them. These markets that manage user data are complicated to understand and involve many business models and people involved in it. [17]The user data holds a high economic value and incentives for the enterprises which makes

it more susceptible towards the concerns of data privacy and its regulations.

One of the most serious jeopardizing acts is the identity theft which poses a serious concern to the consumer. In addition to these other events like loss of data, unapproved data sharing, spam messages and emails, push notifications, tracking of device location, access to contacts and images. The user if agrees to share his data with one business in a particular situation may be exploited by another business in a different context. [18]

Privacy as a part of competition has been discussed over many a times, and many reports by UK Furman Report, CMA Report, OECD Big Data Report, and European Data Protection Supervisor Report, and these reports in a summary mention about the privacy of consumer and the completion law and data connection in it, how the interplay comes in role between the competition law a data privacy. However, it also notes that the privacy is not concerned with the scope of intervention of competition authorities due to the lower cases of consumer data rights.

CHAPTER EIGHT

HOW DATA PRIVACY IS LINKED TO COMPETITION REGULATION

In India the right to privacy was included in the fundamental rights by the Supreme Court of India in 2017. However, the Indian government has established a specialized legislation responsible for the maintenance and management of privacy rights and even set up the "Personal Data Protection Bill, 2019". The bill is expected to enforce the section "43A of IT Act". [21]The definition of personal data as given by PDB is "relating to a natural person who is directly or indirectly identifiable having regard to any characteristic trait attribute or any other feature of the identity of such natural person whether it is offline or online and it shall include any inference drawn from such data for the purpose of profiling". The law is set to show an inclement in the compliance associated needs, which allows the user to have more control on its privacy and information, the law also establishes a regulator to supervise the data protection difficulties ("Data Protection Authority of India") and lays out the rules for data storage and localization of data. In addition to this the personal data protection bill allows the data protection authority for exhibiting some extraterritorial powers and enables them to pose monetary penalties for non-compliance of the bill. Lastly, it exempts the government organizations from some or more clauses of the bill keeping in mind the protection of user's privacy[22].

A separate entity has been formed to report the base work for government in relation to the general data in July 2020 namely MEITY in the NPD Report. General data includes the data which is not related to any personal information and cannot be used to decipher an individual's identity. However, the NPD Report does not align with the principles of the competition act, 2002 and even remarks that competition law is now a means of protection for the competitors. Furthermore, it adds that enterprises with the huge data information pool have outnumbered and pose an unbeatable techno-economic benefit. Due to this many new entrepreneurs and start-ups have suffered badly.

The CCI, is in charge for preventing the practice of such adverse practices that could pose a negative impact on competition in the market. Under the "competition act, 2002" the CCI is responsible for looking over three countenances that are as follows:

• Anti-competitive agreements amongst the industries amid the section 3 of competition act

• According to section 4 of the competition act the industries are not allowed to dominate

• Under the Sections 5 and 6, competition act mergers and acquisitions must be regulated

[24]The role of the competition act in digital privacy and data security could be complicated and also referred to as the zero-revenue generating market. However, this has become outdated and contradictory in today's world amongst the traditional definitions of economic and market theories in competitive harm. Furthermore, the digital market are more complex to limit due to their other unique features involving perplexity in assessing market power or shares, followed by the poor entry barriers for new entrants to either expand or grow in the market. Lastly the consumer complicates it further by being multi home yet being confined as a result of interoperability[25].

The CCI had very recently considered data as an asset although it had been in its inception since 2010. The "CCI Telecom Report released by CCI in January 2021", referring to the telecom sector in India, and taking into account the convergence of data privacy and the competition law. It specifies the use of user data at a non-price competition, pointing that the data set collected from the user may be used as advantageous asset by the enterprises to overcome its competitors. While in a different report published in 2020 the CCI have highlighted towards the effect of collection of large data sets lets the industries compete on a different level and creating a bias system where only the champion receives it all. The data information could be utilized as an asset in establishing the market power, and once the goal is achieved the data information is open to misuse and an adverse effect to the competition.

More Data more power: [26]The WhatsApp and Facebook aka Meta have received an order by "CCI under section 26(1) of the competition act, 2002" to investigate about the non-price competitive parameters of the company (Case name: WhatsApp Suo Motor Order). The order issued by CCI, they noted the policy-making history of the apps used to make its market power and the strategies of use. After conducting the investigation, the CCI concluded that both the apps have a wide popularity and usage, the users enjoy the one-on-one communication and unique features making both WhatsApp and Facebook domineering the market. The CCI statement holds significance which is dependent on the population of its user on the stage creating a network community.

In relation to data privacy and storage, CCI had released previous statements stating that businesses like Meta previously known as Facebook have the potential to gather and operate considerate amounts of user data information. The CCI has moved forward with this theory in its WhatsApp Suo Motor Order stating that the data impelled community, the competition laws should necessitate the examination of exorbitant data collection and the degree to which the data could be collected is either used or shared by the company against the anti-competitive policies, thereby needing anti-trust scrutiny.

Misuse of Supremacy by Data Manipulation:[27]The telecom reports released by CCI indicates the picture of disparaging conduct:

a. Little or no privacy criterion signifying absence of consumer welfare or data safety.

b. Reduce data safety and protection pointing towards the exclusionary behaviour of the companies

c. Using the user data as a business advantage in diverse services

[28]WhatsApp Suo Motor Order, also highlights this theory of damage, and points towards the fact the data is share by both WhatsApp and Facebook leads to a detoriation of the non-price framework of the competition, and this convey leads to use of biased and unfair terms and conditions imposed on the user of these apps. For instance, in the recent update of WhatsApp the users were forced to agree to allow data sharing with Facebook to be able to continue use of the app. This update however raised further questions and unfair means of data privacy.

CHAPTER NINE

FUTURE POSSIBILITIES AND LIMITATIONS OF COMPETITION REGULATION AND COMPETITION LAW IN DATA PRIVACY

[29]The CCI Telecom Reports recognizes the data as a barometer for non-price competition, acknowledging the user privacy could also be in paradigm with the consumer protection issue and the competition law which is focused on conservation and bringing up the competition market rather than protecting each market enterprise including both competitors and consumers.

The CCI should therefore focus on working along with other agencies that pose high value to be able to set boundaries and criterion for data safety and privacy. While the CCI could adapt more knowledge and strategies from the anti-competitive deviation. The CCI could set standards and cognizance from the exorbitant data collection practices and could thereby establish contradictory situations with additional regulators in better situation to create assessment on these events.

In addition, [30]the CCI is yet in developmental stages for creating its position on data safety and protection. The CCI in the past cases have shut down supported on 'bald assertions' and 'affirmations which are neither substantiated in any manner' and has also denied to hold any future exclusion in context to theory of damage. However, the recent investigations on WhatsApp and MMT Interim Order to be supported by uncorroborated statements.

[31]The limits and boundaries of data safety are yet to be established and defined in a more precise manner keeping in mind the recent developments in business digital models and the future possibilities of digital market to create an unbiased and fair market for everyone. The appeals in the high court are also yet to be settled down coupled with the premature knowledge of CCI in investigations and digital market boundaries and scope. The future possibilities for CCI could be improved by being more liberal and thorough in preliminary hearings. It could also elucidate the underlying tech and enterprise models to CCI and optimize the resources which could be potential signs to the CCI in the investigation.

The current modernization needs clear and comprehensive data privacy and safety legislation that could come into action at the earliest to prevent any further misuse and market biasness. The legislation if able to set a limiting value on the user data collection, it would then allow the CCI to further control the market authority in digital space and market. Intriguingly, the MEITY has stepped forward and released an official notification that determines the substantial social media mediator as a social media conciliator with 5 million or more registered users in India. Hereby, the CCI may not release the limiting value for the data set, and rather expand its understanding of the fundamental concerns via market surveys and studies and preparatory conferences and emphasis on an effects-based approach.

The business models in digital market should also review their policy and terms and conditions regarding the safety and welfare of its users. They should be more transparent in data privacy and safety and mention it in advertising as well.

CHAPTER TEN

CONCLUSION

The responsibility of CCI as a body for regulating market competition is a comprehensive body embedded with all sectors of the economy involving those who already possess sectorial regulators. Such establishments are in constant need of upgrades and constant consultations and coordination with other bodies and CCI to keep the harmony maintained in the market. The markets are constantly evolving and changing with changes in time and technology, which makes it more dynamic to handle thereby the regulatory authorities require to be more imperative to allow smooth coordination and cope with the new rules to protect the market as well user's welfare in data privacy. Such collaborative works of regulatory authorities along with new business models will result in greater output in regulating the laws and enforcements in the country.[32] The data in today's time holds significant importance as a competitive value in economic engagement and the functioning of competition agencies is working on an assumption basis to maintain and ensure that the stability of the competition is regulated and efficiently stable. The antitrust law architecture is an important regulatory body to tackle the unscrupulous and consumptive behaviour of influential companies in data accumulation and data storage. A clearer understanding and coordination are needed between the enterprises and the regulating authorities to protect data security keeping in mind the future scope and potential of the digital market. Without the competition regulators, influential companies may take over the digital market and will not allow the expansion of new and small businesses causing harm to the market by creating biasness. Therefore, it is necessary to broaden the scope and limit of competition laws and competition authorities in the digital market.